Ladybird Readers

BBC earth

Dangerous Journeys

Inspired by BBC Earth TV series and
developed with input from BBC Earth
natural history specialists

Contents

Ladybird Readers

Dangerous Journeys

Series Editor: Sorrel Pitts
Written by Anne Collins

LADYBIRD BOOKS

UK | USA | Canada | Ireland | Australia
India | New Zealand | South Africa

Ladybird Books is part of the Penguin Random House group of companies
whose addresses can be found at global.penguinrandomhouse.com.
www.penguin.co.uk   www.puffin.co.uk   www.ladybird.co.uk

Penguin
Random House
UK

First published 2017
001

Text copyright © Ladybird Books Ltd, 2017

All images copyright © BBC, 2014
Except: pages 6, 9, 46, 58, 61 (green turtle);
pages 34–35, 58, 60 (green turtle swimming underwater) all © BBC, 2012
Pages 7, 46, 58, 61 (tiger shark), page 19 (island)
Pages 25, 49, 50 (albatrosses on beach) all images copyright © BBC, 2009

BBC and BBC Earth (word marks and logos) are trade marks of the
British Broadcasting Corporation and are used under licence.
BBC logo © BBC 1996. BBC Earth logo © 2014

Printed in China

A CIP catalogue record for this book is available from the British Library

ISBN: 978–0–241–29891–6

All correspondence to:
Ladybird Books
Penguin Random House Children's
80 Strand, London WC2R 0RL

Picture words

zebra

albatross

barnacle geese

green turtle

lion

crocodile

tiger shark

chick

nest

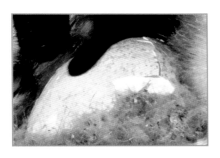

lay (eggs)

(verb)

plains

cliffs

Dangerous journeys

Sometimes, animals make a long or a difficult journey. The journey can be to find food, to run away from other animals or to have babies.

Albatrosses
(island
near Hawaii)

Barnacle geese
(Greenland)

Some animals travel alone, and some travel in groups. Their journeys can often be very dangerous.

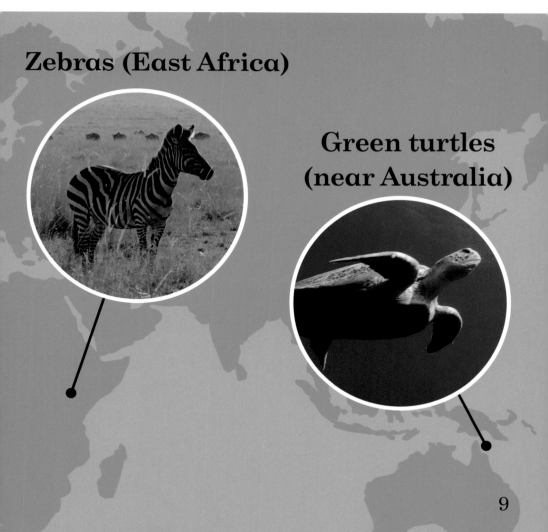

Zebras (East Africa)

Green turtles (near Australia)

Zebras

Zebras eat grass, but when the weather on the plains is very dry, the grass stops growing.

These hungry zebras need to make a journey across a very wide river, because there is more grass to eat on the other side.

plains

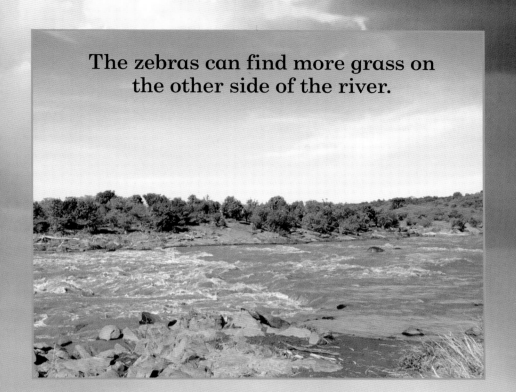

The zebras can find more grass on the other side of the river.

The zebras' journey

The zebras' journey can be very dangerous. This part of the river is very busy with other animals.

There are lots of animals that want to catch and eat the zebras. Two animals that like to eat zebras are lions and crocodiles.

lion

crocodile

Zebras in the river

The zebras go to a quieter part of the river, where there are no lions or crocodiles. But the water here is very fast and strong. This is very dangerous for the zebras.

It is very difficult for this baby zebra to stand in the fast water.

The other side

It is difficult, but finally the zebras get to the other side of the river. The lions and crocodiles have not caught them.

These zebras have crossed safely
to the other side of the river.

Black-footed albatross

The black-footed albatross makes
a nest for its eggs on hot islands
in the north Pacific Ocean.

When albatross chicks have grown big enough, they leave their island and live out on the ocean for a few years. They can fly very far, but starting their journey is the most dangerous part.

An albatross's journey

To leave the island, a young albatross needs to fly.

Its wings are very big. They are 1.83 meters from the end of one wing to the end of the other. This makes it difficult for an albatross to fly up from the ground and stay in the air.

A young albatross tries many times to fly into the air from the beach. But it often comes down into the ocean.

This albatross is
flying into the ocean.

Tiger sharks in the ocean

This part of the journey is very dangerous because there are tiger sharks in the ocean.
The tiger sharks are waiting to catch and eat any albatrosses that come down into
the water!

If an albatross is not caught, it can try to fly away. But it is much more difficult to get back into the air from the water.

tiger shark

This albatross is being caught by a tiger shark.

An ocean journey

This albatross has flown away from a shark. It is strong enough now to make a journey across the ocean.

Later, it will come back to the island to find a partner and make a nest for their chicks.

These young albatrosses will come back to the island to have their chicks.

Barnacle geese

Barnacle geese make their nests and lay eggs on the top of high cliffs in Greenland. Here, they are safe from other animals, but there is no food.

These goose chicks are in their nest.

Soon after the chicks come out of the eggs, they have to make a very dangerous journey, because there is nothing to eat on top of the cliffs.

cliffs

Down the cliffs

The mother and father geese fly down to the bottom of the cliffs and call to their chicks.

Because they are so young,
the chicks cannot fly yet. They
have to jump and fall down the
cliffs to get to their parents. It
is very far for the chicks to fall!

The chicks jump

When the chicks jump, they hold out their wings so that they fall more slowly. But they cannot fly, so it is very dangerous.

The chicks often hit the sides of the cliff or fall badly. It is very easy for them to hurt themselves.

This little chick is falling down the high cliff.

Together again

The mother and father geese wait for the chicks at the bottom of the cliff.

These chicks have come down safely.

The family are together again,
and they go to find food and water.

This chick is safe with its mother.

Green turtles

Green turtles can live for 100 years or more. They usually live in the ocean for their first 25–50 years. A green turtle can find the food it needs in the ocean. But it has to come back to the beach to lay its eggs.

After a green turtle has laid its eggs, it needs to get back to the ocean as soon as it can. Its journey can be very dangerous.

Turtles on the beach

A green turtle knows the ocean very well, but the beach is a different world. It is difficult for a turtle to move around on the beach because its body is so heavy and slow.

This green turtle must get back to the ocean fast. If it is still on the beach in the day, when the sun is strong, it can quickly get too hot. It will not be able to move or get water.

This turtle is getting very hot in the sun.

The turtle is stuck!

The green turtle has had to pull itself over rocks as well as sand, which is very difficult. It cannot move between the rocks.

Turtles need air, so if the ocean comes in and the water goes over the turtle's head when it cannot move, it will die.

This green turtle is trying to climb over the rocks.

Back in the ocean

Luckily, the waves helped to push the green turtle out of the rocks, and it is free to swim away.

The turtle will have to make the same journey to lay more eggs every two to four years.

41

All journeys

Some animals, like zebras and green turtles, make their journeys many times. They need to find food, or keep themselves and their babies safe.

Some animals, like the barnacle goose chicks, and the young albatrosses, only make their journey once, when they are young.

zebras

barnacle goose chick

young albatross

green turtles

Activities

The key below describes the skills practiced in each activity.

Spelling and writing

Reading

Speaking

? Critical thinking

Preparation for the Cambridge Young Learners Exams

1 Look at the pictures. Write the words on the lines. 📖 ✏️

chick   cliffs   egg   grass   nest   plains

1

plains

2

3

4

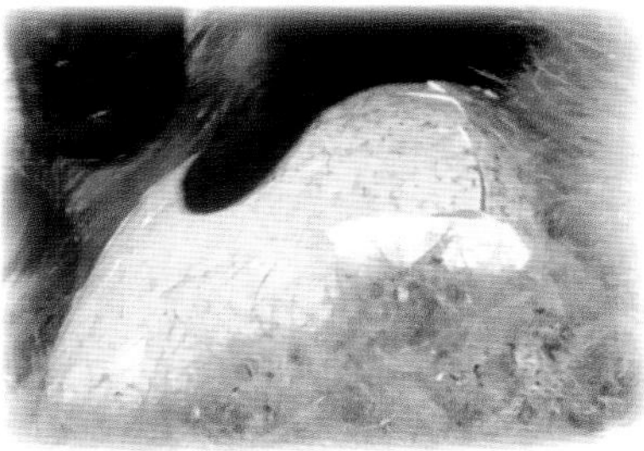

5

6

2 Look, match, and write the words.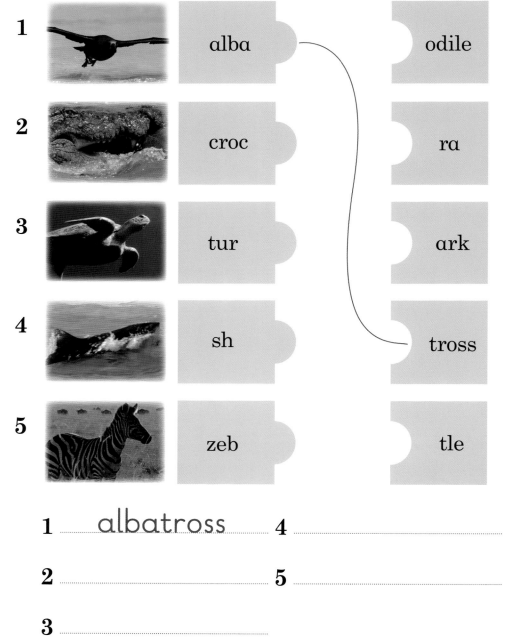

1   alba   odile

2   croc   ra

3   tur   ark

4   sh   tross

5   zeb   tle

1   albatross   4

2   5

3

3 **Read the answers. Write the questions.**

Zebras

Zebras eat grass, but when the weather on the plains is very dry, the grass stops growing.

These hungry zebras need to make a journey across a very wide river, because there is more grass to eat on the other side.

The zebras can find more grass on the other side of the river.

plains

1   What do zebras eat?

They eat grass.

2 Where _____?

On plains in Africa.

3 Why _____?

Because there is more grass on the other side of the river.

4 Why _____?

Because lions and crocodiles want to catch and eat the zebras.

4 **Circle the best answers.**

1 What do zebras eat?

  a They eat grass.

  b They eat meat.

2 Why do zebras make a journey across a river?

  a Because there is more grass to eat on the other side.

  b Because they like swimming.

3 Which animals like to eat zebras?

  a Barnacle geese.

  b Crocodiles and lions.

4 Where is it difficult for a baby zebra to stand?

  a In slow water.

  b In fast water.

5 **Look at the pictures and write the words from the box.** 📖 ✏️

| dangerous   high   hot   wide |

1  These zebras need to make a journey across a .... wide .... river.

2  The black-footed albatross makes a nest for its eggs on .... islands in the north Pacific.

3  This part of the journey is very .... because there are tiger sharks in the ocean.

4  Barnacle geese make their nests on the top of .... cliffs in Greenland.

6 Work with a friend. Talk about the two pictures. How are they different? 💬

a

b

In picture a, there is only one albatross.

In picture b, there are lots of albatrosses.

7 **Look and read. Put a** ✓ **or a** ✗ **in the boxes.** 📖 ⬡

1 This zebra has crossed safely to the other side of the river. ✓

2 This albatross is swimming out of the ocean. ☐

3 It's easy for this turtle to move about on the beach. ☐

4 This little chick is climbing up the high cliff. ☐

5 This albatross is being caught by a tiger shark. ☐

8 Look at the letters. Write the words. 📖 ✏️ 💬

1 (o r j y e n u)

Sometimes, animals must make
a long or a difficult __journey__.

2 (l p n s i a)

When the weather on the ....
is very dry, the grass stops growing.

3 (i n s l o)

Two animals that like to eat zebras
are .... and crocodiles.

4 (e s n t)

The black-footed albatross makes
a .... for its eggs on hot
islands in the north Pacific Ocean.

9 Write *always* or *never*.

1 Barnacle geese _____always_____
make their nests and lay eggs
on the top of high cliffs.

2 Here, they are safe from
other animals, but there is
_____ any food to eat.

3 After the chicks come out of the
eggs, they _____ have to
make a very dangerous journey.

4 The chicks _____ fly
when they are first born, so they
have to jump off the cliffs.

5 The mother and father geese
_____ wait for them
at the bottom of the cliff.

10 **Work with a friend. Ask and answer questions about barnacle geese.**

Barnacle geese

Barnacle geese make their nests and lay eggs on the top of high cliffs in Greenland. Here, they are safe from other animals, but there is no food.

These geese chicks are in their nest

Soon after the chicks come out of the eggs, they have to make a very dangerous journey. There is nothing to eat on top of the cliffs.

26

cliffs

27

Which animals are these?

They are barnacle geese.

11 **Look and read. Choose the correct words and write them on the lines.**

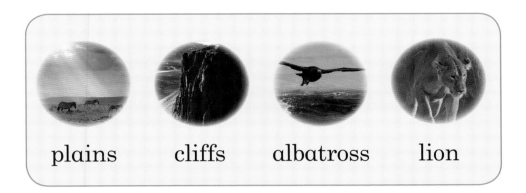

| plains | cliffs | albatross | lion |

1 This is an animal that likes to catch and eat zebras. _lion_

2 This is where zebras live. _____

3 This is a big bird with black feet. _____

4 Barnacle geese make nests on these so they are safe. _____

12 Match the two parts of the sentences.

1 If the zebras don't cross the river

2 If an albatross isn't caught by a tiger shark in the ocean,

3 If the barnacle geese don't leave their nest,

4 If the water goes over the turtle's head when it cannot move,

a it can try to fly away.

b it will die.

c they won't find grass.

d they won't have any food.

13 Look and read. Circle the correct words. 📖

1  Zebras eat grass, but when the weather on the plains is very **(dry)**/ **wet** the grass stops growing.

2  These **angry / hungry** zebras have to make a journey across a very wide river.

3  It is very **difficult / easy** for the baby zebra to stand in the fast water.

4  Barnacle geese make their nests and lay eggs on the top of high cliffs where it is **dangerous. / safe**.

14 **Circle the correct pictures.**

1 This is a dangerous animal.

2 This animal lays eggs.

3 This is where the barnacle geese make their nests.

  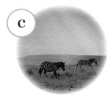

4 These help you fly high and far.

15 **Read the text. Choose the correct words and write them on the lines.**

1 make	makes	to make
2 are growing	have grown	has grown
3 can fly	can flying	can to fly

The black-footed albatross

[1] _____makes_____ a nest for its

eggs on hot islands in the north Pacific

Ocean. When albatross chicks

[2] _____ big enough, they

leave their island and live out on the

ocean. They [3] _____

very far, but starting their journey is

the most dangerous part.

16 **Look and read. Write the correct words.** 📖 ✏️

1  Green turtles usually live ~~on the beach~~.

in the ocean

2  They have to come back to the beach to lay their ~~chicks~~.

....

3  This turtle is getting very ~~cold~~ in the sun.

....

4  Luckily, the waves have helped to push the green turtle out of the rocks, and she is free to ~~walk~~ away.

....

17 Look and read. Write *yes* or *no*.

  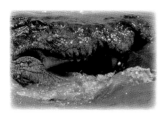

1 Zebras like to eat lions
and crocodiles. ....no........

2 There are tiger sharks
in the Pacific Ocean. ....

3 Barnacle geese make
their nests on the top
of high cliffs. ....

4 Green turtles usually
live on the beach. ....

18 Write the missing letters.

ss   ee   ff   ck   ea

1   c l i _f_ _f_

2   c h i ___ ___

3   g ___ ___ s e

4   b ___ ___ c h

5   g r a ___ ___

19 Read and write the correct form of the verbs.

All journeys

Some animals, like zebras and green turtles, make their journeys many times. They need to find food, or keep themselves and their babies safe.

Some animals, like the barnacle goose chicks, and the young albatrosses, only make their journey once, when they are young.

barnacle goose chick

young albatross

zebras

green turtles

42   43

Some animals, like zebras and green turtles, ¹ _will need_ **(need)**, to make their journeys many times ² _____ **(find)** food, or ³ _____ **(keep)** themselves and their babies safe. Some animals, like the Barnacle goose chicks and the young albatrosses, only ⁴ _____ **(make)** their journey once, when they ⁵ _____ **(be)** young.

63

Level 4

The Pied Piper of Hamelin

978–0–241–25378–6 ☐

The Wizard of Oz

978–0–241–25379–3 ☐

Sam and the Robots

978-0-241-25380-9 ☐

The Little Mermaid

978-0-241-29874-9 ☐

Space

978–0–241–25381–6 ☐

Pinocchio

978–0–241–28430–8 ☐

Alice in Wonderland

978–0–241–28431–5 ☐

Under the Oceans

978-0-241-29888-6 ☐

Knights and Castles

978–0–241–28432–2 ☐

Heidi

978–0–241–28433–9 ☐

Peter and the Wolf

978–0–241–28434–6 ☐

Dangerous Journeys

978–0–241–29891–6 ☐

A Fight with Underbite

978-0-241-29890-9 ☐

Sideswipe Loses his Head

978-0-241-29889-3 ☐